Let Not Your Heart Be Troubled:

A Healing Guide for Black Women

By Rev. Dr. Lisa D. Robinson

Copyright © Rev. Dr. Lisa D. Robinson

ISBN: 978-1-952327-51-3
Library of Congress Control Number: 2021903077

Title: Let Not Your Heart Be Troubled: A Healing Guide for Black Women

Scripture quotations are from New Revised Standard Version of the Bible, copyright © 1946, 1952, and 1971 National Council of the Churches of Christ in the United States of America. Used by permission. All rights reserved worldwide.

Names and details have been modified to reflect the authors creative intent.

All rights reserved. No part of this book may be reproduced or transmitted in any form or by any means without written permission from the author.

T.A.L.K. Publishing
5215 North Ironwood Road, Suite 200
Glendale, WI 53217
talkconsulting.net

Dedication

*In loving memory of my father and brother,
and to my loving mother, daughter, siblings, extended
family, ancestors, colleagues, and friends around the world.*

and

*To all the Black women who see themselves
reflected in these stories.*

To God be the Glory!

Table of Contents

1. God is a God of Justice 9
2. Love as You Want to Be Loved 15
3. Joy After Pain 21
4. Deliver Us From Evil 27
5. A Steadfast and Immovable Spirit 33
6. Bless Those Who Curse You 41
7. For God's Glory 45
8. It is Well 51
9. God Watches Over Me 55
10. Passion for Justice 65
11. Anger in the Valley 69
12. God Has Prepared a Place 75
13. Lord, I Look to You 81
14. Make Room at Your Banquet 89
15. Our Hope is in Christ 97

16.	The Lord Hears the Cry of the Poor	101
17.	When God Sends Angels	105
18.	Don't Pass Me By	113
19.	Death Still Has No Sting	117
20.	A Poetic Justice Hymn	125

God is a God of Justice

"Happy are those who observe justice, who do righteousness at all times." Psalm 106:3

"All rise. Hear ye, hear ye. The court is now in session. Is it true you were in Rock Creek Park, Ms. Johnson?" My mind faded to the rhythm in my head, hearing the lyrics from the hit record-"Rock Creek Park." This silent rhythm caused my foot to tap lightly and my head to slightly bob up and down, hopefully unnoticed. They told all of us, interns, not to make any distracting facial expressions, to try not to move, and to look natural, whatever that meant. This trial was conducted in a courthouse in Washington DC, the nation's capital, not on the Perry Mason legal drama show's re-runs. Here I was officially sitting in the court with an official intern badge, behind the defense attorney, along with 14 of my peers. The room was so tense that none of us dare move intentionally.

They said that to move, laugh or comment without permission meant that the judge could remove us for contempt of court. You didn't have to tell us twice — we knew this was serious. The plaintiff had accused the defendant of rape, and it was clear that somebody was going to pay dearly for this alleged crime. It was dead silence as the defense attorney barked his questions at Ms. Johnson. But as we discussed in our small legal class the next day, the prosecuting attorney sure knew his craft. It was clear that he played a pivotal role in directing his client's demeanor, appearance and dress. As the defense attorney yelled at Ms. Johnson, she remained poised in a pure white dress with white shoes, innocently brushing her blond hair out of her face with her neatly manicured hands. Each time she paused briefly and gulped as if on cue as if she was innocent and scared for her life before responding to his questions.

The whole scene was like a chess game. The defense attorney barked; the plaintiff played innocent, and the music in my head continued, "Doing it in the park, doing it after dark, oh yeah, Rock Creek Park, oh yeah, Rock Creek Park." Before, this was just a song that we bopped our heads to during high school at the local recreation center parties and in the community parks on the playground. Now, these lyrics took on an entirely new meaning. Answer the question, Ms.

Johnson, were you in Rock Creek Park on the night of..." Soon, the judge called for a recess. We were all hooked at that point. Like everyone else gathered in the courtroom on that day, we wanted to know who was innocent or guilty? The blond defendant's contrast juxtaposed against her alleged black boyfriend and his associates, his "homies," coupled with the charge of rape was more than a date gone wrong. Instead, a similar scene played out many times in America where black men, white women, and the law would not always have a happy ending. Since the days of slavery and lynching, many black men have been killed, hung, and brutally beaten for interacting with white women. Eerily, this day in court brought up images of our racist history. Unfortunately, we left before the judge issued a verdict, and I left feeling that there was something more to this story. While growing up, I remember the old saying that there were two sides to every story-- and somewhere in the middle lies the truth. Maybe she was innocent; perhaps she wasn't.

Maybe he was innocent. Perhaps he wasn't. I knew one thing. If anybody knows what happened that night in Rock Creek Park, God knows. But what if that was me, a woman of color, a black woman in Rock Creek Park? Would I be allowed to wear a white dress and claim my innocence, represented by one of D.C.'s finest attorneys? Who knows? But years later, this case strongly resonated with me as I had the opportunity to research, design, and teach a new women's studies class at the University. Is it any wonder that I chose to name it—"Women of Color and the Legal System?" And sadly, our class discussed a similar story of a young white woman and her black boyfriend. It was almost the same situation. This time, however, it wasn't rape but drug and gun charges, and this time the young woman admitted that the drugs and gun were hers but that she couldn't bring herself to tell that to the police. In tears, she realized that she went free and was graduating college while her black boyfriend and his buddy, on the other hand, were both serving time-based on her lie. What the class learned from this experience is that everything is not always as it seems. Innocent people die. While money can't always buy love, it can undoubtedly destroy lives when racism and classism rear their ugly heads in a deeply entrenched, dysfunctional, and biased system of law.

Key Takeaways:
- Everything is not always Black and White.
- Others may judge you, but God is the ultimate judge.
- Hold on to God's Promises; the truth will make you free.

Prayer:
Sovereign Lord, please give us the wisdom and strength to stand on Your Word. For You are the way, the truth, and the life, and you are a God of justice. May we turn from evil and seek your ways always. We ask this in the name of Jesus, our Lord. Amen.

Love as You Want to Be Loved

"Love does no wrong to a neighbor; therefore, love is the fulfilling of the law." Romans 13:10

Sitting on the bench outside of the Martin Luther King Jr. Memorial Library on the Northwest side of Washington, DC, I just wanted some heat after being inside the big air-conditioned building. It may have been a heatwave outside in this sweltering D.C. summer, but inside, it felt like the North Pole, at least to me. Even the goosebumps on my arms felt like they needed a space heater. I thought a little break in the sunshine would do me good before I headed back to marvel at the thousands of books in this beautiful and historical library.

My fetish with books had gotten a hold of me this Saturday morning. I appreciated being a part of this prestigious program with 300 other students selected from around the country. Our schedule was packed every day, from juggling our 35 hours/week responsibilities at our assigned agency to sitting through seminars and taking classes with high power and well-known political and business leaders. This hectic schedule occurred throughout the week and into the evening hours. We had large and small gatherings with U.S. Senators and Congressional members, legislative assistants, CEOs, and some of the most wealthy and well-connected individuals in the country. In between, we engaged in one on ones with our assigned mentors, worked in our small cohort groups, and took in as many happy hours that we could. We collectively became adept at finding every free buffalo wing, hors d'oeuvres, and complimentary dinner specials inside the D.C. beltway. So, when I finally did get time for a personal break, away from this hectic schedule, I knew that I wanted to visit the famous MLK Library. Carefully crossing the street, I plopped down on the bench a stone's throw away from the library. Soon an older black man made his way to the same bench. He questioned why I was there in the library on a Saturday afternoon.

 I quickly glanced at him and couldn't help but notice the faint smell of liquor on his breath and his hand clutching something in this pocket. Before I could adequately respond to his uninvited comment, he proceeded to "preach" that "had I studied a little harder, I wouldn't have to spend my summer days in summer school." He further added, "That's what's wrong with young Blacks today" and walked off mumbling, pushing his bottle in his pants pocket. I tried to make sense of what he said, realizing that he prejudged me without even knowing me. How indignant of him. How dare he assume that I was in summer school, trying to make-up failed classes. Had he taken the time to await my response, I might have enlightened him that I graduated high school early with honors, was on the dean's list at college, and was preparing to graduate in a few months to attend graduate school.

On further reflection, I dismissed his comment as being his problem, not mine. What if I had been a dropout? What if I had failed my class? Would that warrant someone looking down on me if I had? Doesn't the Bible say to be kind and loving? Who knows what motivated him to single me out with such disdain in his voice.

On the other hand, who knows what happened to him before sitting on that bench; maybe he had personal problems. He had been drinking liquor; the smell lingered in the air, some clinging to my clothing. I could have retaliated and commented on his "drinking habit."

LOVE AS YOU WANT TO BE LOVED

But what would that have accomplished? Maybe he was covering up his past pain and hurt with his liquor. I will probably never find out, but I decided to cling to my biblical upbringing by remembering that I am a child of the 'Most High' God. Every negative comment doesn't warrant a return comment. Too much negative energy can take your focus off of God and place it on man. But the Bible tells us to be wise as a serpent. The Bible also tells us to judge not, or you'll be judged. And the Bible says love as we want to be loved and to pray for and forgive others. As a young intern in D.C., the first time away from home on my own, I soon learned that this summer would be a journey filled with unexpected twists and turns, which would eventually become life-long lessons. As I walked back across the street and into the cold library, I just thanked the Lord that God would be by my side.

Key Takeaways:
- Forgive others for Christ has forgiven you.
- It may be hard to extend patience or grace to those who harm or hurt us, but it is necessary.
- Like Jesus, pray for forgiveness — for none of us are perfect.

Prayer:
Loving God, we pray for those who despise us at times. Fill us with a well of love that never runs dry. May there be a dawning of new believers who remember to be caring and kind-hearted even when it hurts. Amen.

Joy After Pain

"But those who wait for the Lord shall renew their strength, they shall mount up with wings like eagles, they shall run and not be weary, they shall walk and not faint."
Isaiah 40:31

As I lay in the maternity ward in a lot of pain, I recall my mother saying it felt like fire when she delivered my twin sister and me in what now seemed like another lifetime. The more I tossed and turned, the more painful it became. I just couldn't find a comfortable position. Several nursing staff came in and out of my room, doing their best to comfort me and bring me crackers and water. The doctor had said he would be back and not to worry, "your baby should be here soon." That was last night, close to the midnight hour. It was now lunchtime, and he had already told me that at breakfast time, "not to worry, your baby will be here soon," he said with a smile as he left, closing the large hospital door behind him.

This situation certainly did not look like the pregnancy I saw on television where the mother rushes to the hospital, in minutes has the baby. In the next scene, she is happily coddling her newborn wrapped in a clean blanket. No, I only knew pain, and I only felt that "fire" my mother had described with our birth experience. Tossing and turning in pain, falling in and out of sleep, I just wished it was all over. I wanted the scene with my new baby wrapped in the clean, soft blanket in my arms to hurry up and come. This waiting took too long, and I bargained with God about, "why me and why now?" I know in the Bible God says to Eve after she eats the forbidden fruit, "I will greatly multiply your sorrow and your conception; In pain, you shall bring forth children;" ... but I wasn't Eve, and this pain was becoming unbearable, and all I wanted was a relief. After drifting off to sleep again, I was awakened by the same doctor and another of his colleagues. Together they assured me that everything was fine and that they were there to administer pain relief, an epidural in my back. Immediately after they injected my body, I screamed out in pain, and the looks on their face assured me that everything wasn't fine. As they hurriedly left the room, I heard the main doctor in a concerned voice say to his colleague something like, "you weren't supposed to do it like that." The door closed, and I wasn't privy to any more of their conversation; I just knew I was in more pain, and I knew something wasn't right. Help me God is all I could think. As the clock ticked, more doctors and nurses came in, and they told me they would rush me down the hall for emergency surgery. An emergency?

What happened to everything would be alright? What happened to your baby will be here soon? For the next few minutes, all I could see were white coats and scrubs, doctors, nurses, and tech assistants scurrying to their assigned tasks. The beeps on the medical devices, the IV tubes in my arms, and codes coming from the hospital P.A. system were loud and distracting, but they were not loud or distracting to the point to keep me from remembering all the pain I was experiencing. For me, the fire and the excruciating pain had now reached my description of Code Red. "O God, O God, I cried, "please stop this pain!" Before I knew it, they transferred me to another hospital bed prepped for emergency surgery. Doctors determined that the baby could not be born vaginally due to health concerns. They opted to perform an emergency cesarean section instead. All of a sudden, I could feel them cutting through my abdomen. The medication was working

JOY AFTER PAIN

because I no longer felt pain, but I did feel the heavy pressure of what seemed like someone taking a saw and cutting deep across my belly.

In what seemed like minutes, I saw them raise a baby in the air, and in seconds she was taken away with the message to me that something was wrong but, "not to worry, you will see your baby again soon."

"Not to worry? I will see my baby, again?" I barely saw her for a second before they whisked her away and ran with her down the hall. So, no, there was no baby wrapped in a clean, soft blanket handed to me after birth.

And no, everything would not be alright. Twelve hours later, a nurse wheeled me down the hall to see Laci Nicole Robinson. Ignoring my pain from the traumatic surgery, I reunited with my new bundle of joy. This meeting was not the type of bonding that I anticipated, but it was the beginning of a lifelong bond that God had already preordained. Here she was at 8lbs, 6 oz, and 19 inches long, lying peacefully in an incubator wrapped with several tubes attached to her little body. The Hydrocephalus medical diagnoses, i.e., water on the brain, would now become a fixture in our lives. Until the foreseeable future, doctors, nurses, medical appointments, and educational challenges would become our new norm.

But for now, the nurses had already started to treat her with special care and affection. Her big eyes, beautiful smile, and even-tempered personality radiated a presence that seemed to draw people to her naturally. Like baby Jesus, she wasn't born in wealth and riches, but she would grow to become a light in the world in her unique way. Throughout this ordeal, I had wondered what had happened to my regular OB/GYN, the friendly doctor who had monitored my progress since I found out I was pregnant.

I thought it was great that although she was also pregnant that she took the time to care for all of her patients with such compassion. After I returned home, my answer came. She called and relayed that she went into labor the same night, but unfortunately, her baby was stillborn and didn't survive.

She respectfully requested that the medical staff not share this information with me while going through my ordeal to spare me any agony. I thanked her kindly for sharing this information and let her know that I was praying for her. We both hung up, and I thanked God for the gift of life.

Key Takeaways:
- Through the pain and suffering, God is always there.
- Be grateful because someone always has it worse than you.
- Our blessings may not show up in the way that we planned, but they're still a gift from God.

Prayer:
Dear Father God, thank you for the wonderful gift of life. You continue to shower your blessings on us even with our shortcomings. May you cover our children in prayer and hold them safe in your loving arms. We bless your name forever and ever. Amen.

Deliver Us From Evil

"When he was abused, he did not return abuse; when he suffered, he did not threaten, but he entrusted himself to the one who judges justly." 1 Peter 2:23

Who can forget the unforgettable evening of March 3, 1991, the night a bystander videotaped a gang of Los Angeles police officers beating Rodney King, a young, 25-year-old African American man? This riveting video became the 20th-century symbol of racial injustice in America. Each kick, club, and assault on his body was a clear reminder that racism in America was alive and well. It was a reminder that what Dr. Martin Luther King so courageously advocated for was being viciously kicked out on the bloody streets of L.A.

Millions watched in horror as police brutally beat King's body like a rag doll on the cement ground. Unbeknownst to the perpetrators, however, this "beat down" would not go unnoticed. Someone was secretly videotaping this horrific crime. Within hours, anger, tears, and feelings of disgust rolled across America's landscape as the video showed up on televisions in homes, bars, and college campuses, from the cities to the suburbs. If Dr. King's dream of having his little children one day live in an environment where they won't be judged by their skin color but by the content of their character was on the brink of being realized, it was quickly shut down by each kick to Rodney King's bloody body that night. If Rodney's videotaped assault was initially dismissed in court, leading to massive riots, then it was no surprise when my assault about the same time, about the same night, was also quickly dismissed. It was in this moment that I felt my life was standing between two Kings.

"Did you have any witnesses? Did anybody hear you scream" my attorney asked as he hurriedly jotted notes on the faded yellow legal pad on his desk. Without any witnesses, he solemnly told me, there is not much he could legally do. It was 1991, the legal system he nervously explained hadn't made it clear that a family matter could be considered an assault. As anger swelled up inside of me, I began to try to make sense of what he was saying. As the warm tears rolled down my face, I became numb. In 1991, was this attorney who I just paid a retainer telling me that it was okay for a husband to assault his wife? Was he telling me that it would be easier to file a legal report if this man had been a stranger, someone off the street, rather than the one I took vows with-in sickness and health, till death we do part? As he kept flipping nervously through his legal manuals trying to find a way to fix this messed up system while diverting eye contact, all he could ask me was if I had a witness? My 5-year-old was a witness who watched as her father swung with all his might landing his fist in my right eye. Who knew that blow would blind me for life? Who knew that his 10-minute visit barging into the house to complain about my divorce filing papers would rip me of my God-given sight, my 20/20 vision? It happened so quickly. I sat at the kitchen table eating my dinner as my daughter quietly watched television when he entered the house. The court papers removed him from home but still gave him weekly access to visit his daughter. Yet, visiting his daughter was the last thing on his mind on this unforgettable night. He came with a vengeance in his heart and on a mission to destroy whatever was in his path. The demand to sign his handwritten papers fell on deaf ears because I had already had formal reports typed up and sent to my divorce attorney, who filed them with the court. I just ignored his rants. When the papers, however, came ricocheting across my plate and hitting me in the chest, I immediately stood up only to be confronted with a fist in my eye. He immediately ran out of the house, hopped in his car, and drove off like a mad man. Unlike Rodney, there were not 15 officers pounding on my body. There were no baton clubs and swift kicks and racial epithets hurled around. And there was certainly no one secretly videotaping this horrific assault. Ten minutes of horror and my world came crashing down. At that moment, I wanted vengeance. Part of me wanted to retaliate with the same pain he inflicted on me. But there was no time for that. Excruciating pain, blood swelled eye, facial bruises, and uncontrollable rage, and tears came rolling down. Lord, if I ever needed you, I need you now. Where was the peace that Dr. King fought for in the movement? This violence could not be it. This house was a black household in a predominantly white Midwestern town. Do I dare call the police? Do I dare call another Pastor? The first two African American Pastors I called were sexist to the core. Later, the white male nurse at the hospital was just as problematic as the pastors. So, no, I refused and called my mother. Like Rodney King later questioned to America, "Can't we all get along?" Obviously, no, but by God's grace, I would now see life differently through a different lens. These 10 minutes of horror set me up for a life's journey of giving voice to women around the world. I would soon have many opportunities to relay messages to women to trust in the Lord with all their heart and all their mind. Through it all, I thank God for the Word, "And lead us not into temptation, but deliver us from evil: For thine is the kingdom, and the power and the glory, forever. Amen."

Key Takeaways:
- Don't let anger take root.
- Trials will come when least expected, but God's mercy is sufficient.
- Your Witness and Protector is in Heaven.

Prayer:
Merciful God, we pray for discernment to make wise choices. Lead us to know that we can trust your guiding hand. O God, help me find compassion and cradle forgiveness in my heart and remind me the battle is not mine; it's yours. Amen.

A Steadfast and Immovable Spirit

"Therefore, my beloved, be steadfast, immovable, always excelling in the work of the Lord because you know that in the Lord, your labor is not in vain."
1 Corinthians 15:58

"Have a nice day, Lay." "Okay, Mommy." I watched as she walked into the building hurrying to her second-grade class with the other walkers whose parents had dropped them off at school. At this time, neither of us knew that this would be one of her final days at this school. God already knew that we would be leaving in the next couple of months to begin a new chapter of our life with new friends and new schools in a new environment. Yet neither of us had any clue about this new pending adventure that awaited us very shortly. Driving out of the circle and back onto the main road, I couldn't help but notice how brightly the sun was shining through the front window. Within minutes a loud bang brought me out of my reminiscing moments.

As my body jerked back and forth, I realized I had hit something. The car in front of me had come to a complete halt. It was then that I realized I had just had an accident. After taking a moment to compose myself, I opened my car door and quickly approached the driver's side to see if he or she was okay. Upon reaching the car, I said to the driver, "Are You alright?" He looked at me and, without answering, yelled, "My back, my back, you ran into me. My back, my back." Since I never had an accident before, this initially made me have compassion for this man. If I was at fault, then I wanted to make sure he was okay and deal with the consequences later. I paused to pray for him. This compassion, however, did not last long. When I asked him if I could help, his tone became very arrogant. He first said to his son under his breath (thinking I couldn't hear him), "go and call 911." The seven or 8-year-old paused and then looked up at his father, who only became more irate and yelled at him, "I said get out of this car, run over there, and call 911." The frightened young man flew out of the car, appearing to be obedient and scared at the same time.

This interaction between father and son irked me for two reasons. First, he demeaned his son, and secondly, because the whole scenario now seemed like a set-up. Within seconds of yelling at his son, he turned to look back towards me and strategically put his hand on his back again, crying, "My back, my back, you ran into me, my back, my back." After this little charade, he convinced me that he faked his injuries. I felt sorry for his son and silently prayed for him, but simultaneously knew the father was setting me up. It wouldn't be until a couple of weeks later that I would soon find out the absolute truth, the con game, and the nationwide scam that he pulled me into as an unwilling player. On the other hand, he would later find out that crime doesn't pay and that God sees all.

Not too long after this accident, I left town to begin my doctoral program in Massachusetts. As grad school continued, this case sort of disappeared into the background. A few years later, I was now heavily into my research and had received a fellowship that took me to live in Washington State for the summer.

However, through conversations with the insurance company, I already found out that this man was under investigation with the National Insurance Crime Bureau for possible fraud. He had successfully sued two other people in what the insurance company shared with me was a scheme called "Crash for Cash" or Staged Rear-Ending." My suspicions were correct. I did run into him, but that was because he purposely stopped so that I would hit his car and so that he could claim he was injured.

His fraudulent scheme worked in his favor in the past; he went so far as to have his attorney send me a letter suing me $10,000 for his injuries and $10,000 for his son's injuries. I mean, really, the little boy who he yelled at to run across the street to call 911?

I know God would have to intervene in this situation because it was so beyond me that someone could do something so stupid and involve his child in it just to get some quick money. I went back to focusing on my fellowship on the other side of the country, and the committee selected thirteen of us from more than 100 applicants. We were all African American doctoral students from different states and various postgraduate programs, one male and 12 females. This fellowship program was going to be an intense summer and an interesting one as well. I refused to let a scammer steal my joy. The very first night, my assigned mentor, a young white faculty mentor, picked me up from the airport. She filled me in on the internship expectations, told me about exciting things to do in the area, and shared good places to eat. I was tired and sleepy from the long plane ride from the East coast but tried my best to keep track of everything she told me. Then as we pulled up to the dorm where I would be staying, she slowed the car down, and her voice took on another tone. As she bid me farewell, she said in a very cautious and concerned manner to be very careful and try to avoid a particular area because that's where many skinheads and members of the Neo-Nazis, Aryan Nations, and other hate groups tended to hang out. To myself, I'm thinking, Skinheads and hate groups? I grew up 5 minutes outside of N.Y., and cowards who hated black people didn't faze me. But I thanked her for her concern, went inside, and quickly dozed off to sleep. Gratefully, the summer went fine. The fellowship was a great experience, and just as I forgot about the man who was scamming me, I also forgot about her comment about the skinheads and the other hate groups.

Well, at least for the time being, they all became figments of my imagination. In the last week of my program, however, as I packed up to head back to the East coast, I opened up a piece of mail my mother had forwarded to me from home. It was a formal letter from the insurance company. As I read the contents, it brought a smile to my face. "Hallelujah, thank you, Jesus!" The judge dismissed the case. While I was in Washington State, another man who the scammer tried to defraud came forward. He was a white medical doctor who the scammer also accused of running into him and his son. He sued the doctor $10,000 for the scammer's fake injuries and $10,000 for his son's alleged injuries. The insurance company told me the doctor was furious. What the scammer didn't know, however, was that the National Insurance Crime Bureau had intended to use my case to bring him up on fraud charges. Later, when the medical doctor was somehow made aware of my case, he wanted to make sure the scammer got what he deserved. In the end, I don't know what legally happened to the scammer, but I do know that God works on Gods' time, and I had more important things to worry about, including finishing my dissertation.

Months later, after I got back home to Massachusetts, I came across an article in a popular Black magazine. I know it was no coincidence when I casually flipped it open to a small story about a mother and son who got lost and ended up in the wrong neighborhood fearing for their lives. They ended up in

Coeur d'Alene, Idaho, the same city across the state border that my mentor told me to avoid while I was in Washington. I don't recall if these haters physically harmed this mother and son, but I remember it wasn't a pleasant experience.

I was glad that they at least lived to tell their story. Once again, I knew that God was my shield and protector. My colleagues and I could have also easily ended up lost in one of those neighborhoods, but God had other plans.

Key Takeaways:
- Comfort those in trouble.
- Pray for those who hurt you.
- Look to God in trying situations.

Prayer:
Holy Spirit, Help us to lean on you in times of trouble. We thank you for helping us see the good in all people and pray for those who may cause us harm. In You alone will I trust and be eternally grateful. We ask this of you, for you are a merciful God. Amen.

Bless Those Who Curse You

"Keep your tongue from evil and your lips from speaking deceit." Psalm 34:13

Eeny, meeny, miny, moe, Catch an "N" by the toe? I had heard the version of "catch a piggy or a tiger by the toe" when I was younger, but this was the first time I heard of someone using the "N" word to help finish this rhyme. But this one word is what sparked a huge racial uproar on campus. A 65-year-old cafeteria worker behind the counter reportedly completed this rhyme by interrupting the conversation between 2 young black males. They stated that their discussion was solely a private one between the two of them as one of them sang the jingle while trying to decide what he was going to eat—hamburgers, French fries, or chicken? The white 65-year-old woman claimed innocence due to her age growing up in the era of segregation. The two African American undergrad students claimed racism and demanded the University take action. Unfortunately for the University, this incident came on the heels of another racial incident on campus. A young African American student walked into the campus store to purchase something but went into his pocket and pulled out something to eat. The store security immediately accused him of stealing the item, pulled him into the back room, and searched him for allegedly shoplifting. Eventually, they cleared him, but these two incidents back to back caused the whole campus to undergo mandatory diversity training. As one of the lead diversity trainers on campus, I knew this was like a kettle pot getting ready to explode. My plate was already full. During this period, other incidents of racism, sexism, and other forms of discrimination on campus would soon surface, and this was just the beginning.

Key Takeaways:
- Build others up-don't resort to name-calling, teasing, bullying, etc.
- Let the words which flow from your mouth be pleasant.
- Make a habit not to belittle anyone else.

Prayer:

Lord, you know the pain of the afflicted. May we find comfort in your Word when we are the target of someone's harmful acts. We pray that you give us the discernment to separate hate from love and guide us to always lean on the side of love. Amen.

For God's Glory

"Whatever your task, put yourselves into it, as done for the Lord and not for your masters," Colossians 3:23

"Sorry, we are closed," the store manager said with a grimace as he quickly closed the door shut. We kept walking but to no avail because all we kept seeing were closed signs posted in store windows and blinds closed as we passed by the shops and businesses. This was a long trip from Western Massachusetts to Philly, the City of Brotherly Love. I still had my metal key to the city, tucked away in my jewelry box, which I had bought while on my elementary class trip to this city. But it certainly didn't feel like brotherly love right now. Some of us were starving, some of us were exhausted, and many of us just wanted to use a restroom to freshen up. We weren't expecting this backlash so soon into our trip. It felt like we were in the 1950s in the Deep South during Jim Crow Days for a brief second. But this wasn't the 1950's, this was the 1990's, and supposedly we were living in a time where we were free. The closing of their doors in our faces was symbolic of the "whites only" signs on the water fountains and restrooms in years gone by. These were reminders that freedom comes with a price. We were reminded that our version of freedom didn't mean the same thing to those shop owners closing their stores in the middle of the day. We realized that this wasn't any typical day but the day of the Million Woman March, where women traveled to Philly from all over the world to protest injustices inflicted upon women of color since slavery. My colleague, "Keisha," and I, another doctoral student, took it upon ourselves to organize this trip, loading up four busloads of fired-up female students and community members. We knew it was one thing to organize a protest on campus and an entirely different thing to join thousands of other women in a national protest. The trip down from Massachusetts on the turnpike was filled with protest songs, chants, and prayers for change in a land that still placed black women at the bottom of the totem pole. Deep in our hearts, we pledged to show up in full force, for we knew if some of us weren't free, then none of us would really be free either. The march happened after the Civil Rights Movement but way before the Me

Too Movement, before the Black Lives Movement, and before the Stay Woke Movement. It was a follow-up protest to Minister Farrakhan's peaceful and effective Million Man March 2 years prior. The main difference is that the center of attention wasn't placed on national celebrities and high-profile leaders, but rather centered on the everyday Black woman who was just sick and tired of being sick and tired. Almost two hundred of us packed the four buses in solidarity for this national cause. We were determined to march for peace. We were determined to march for change, and we were determined to march out of love and respect for our community. We were tired of hearing about another black woman being killed or assaulted. We were leery of the power structure, saying our turn was coming. We were fed up with a system that shortchanged our paychecks, discounted us in the hiring process, and stripped us of our humanity and dignity in faulty characterizations in every form of media. We were sickened by a society that systemically killed our families and neighbors in the dysfunctional prison, education, and other societal institutions and even on the streets. Many of us learned from the Civil Rights Movement that with no struggle, there's no progress. We knew change wouldn't happen overnight. But we knew change could happen. I recall thousands of us marching and protesting, effectively closing down the main street in front of Rutgers' campus center. In 1985, during my senior year, we participated in hunger strikes and listened to Rev. Jesse Jackson and others lead chants of "End Apartheid Now" from the podium. The words from previous powerful speakers such as Dick Gregory, Gil Scott Heron, and Betty Shabazz throughout my undergraduate years right now rang like marching orders in our ears. Subsequently, Rutgers was one of the first public educational institutions in the United States to successfully divest its endowment of corporations doing business in South Africa. So, I had no doubt change could happen; I just knew it would be on God's time. And so, we left our corporate jobs, teaching positions, community agency positions, parenting obligations, and whatever else tied us to our daily routines to make this trip with our sisters. The act of shutting the doors when we arrived was like a slap in the face but as the song said, We ain't gonna let nobody turn us around, turn us around...." In the bible, the Israelites marched around the city of Jericho. On that seventh day, they got up at daybreak and marched seven times just as they did before, except the final time they circled the city seven times.

This was when Joshua told them that the Lord had given them the city. We, too, were waiting to hear that the Lord has given us the city, and not just Philly but whichever city we came from all over the country. The local newspaper articles, the national press coverage, and the relationships that developed due to our trek to Philly cemented in our hearts that we are strong and mighty in number. Hearing all the powerful speakers, engaging in powerful conversations, and marching in unison with our sisters had us believing that our hearts and minds were on fire, for the Lord. We left feeling energized and rejuvenated. More importantly, we left believing in God's Word that we and our sisters, as a people, are and were "fearfully and wonderfully made."

Key Takeaways:
- Stay the course; there will be challenges and opposition.
- Remain Faithful-do it for God, not man.
- Your work is not in vain.

Prayer:
Thank you, God, for being our protector. Help us to remember that you are still in control. Help us press on and order our steps in your word and remind us not to do anything out of selfish ambition. In the mighty name of Jesus. Amen.

It is Well

"God is our refuge and strength,
a very present help in trouble." Psalm 46:1

I was thrilled. It would be the first day of teaching a Women's Studies Introductory class of 300 students in a lecture hall at the University. The week before, the News and Media Relations department publicly announced in the newspaper, "More than four dozen new tenured, tenure-track, part-time, and visiting faculty members will be on board at the University when classes begin Sept. 8" It was an honor to be selected. I was excited to teach Black Women and Activism, Women of Color and the Legal System, and the highly engaging Introductory Women's Studies class. Listed among these new hires, I saw my name and knew the last year of my doctoral program was about to take a big turn. It was too late to change my mind now; I had already committed to this assignment. Yet, somehow, I knew God would help me juggle research, teaching, parenting, community work, and activism. That's how I made it thus far; why should things be any different now?

As I imagined how this first class would go, my thoughts were interrupted by the phone ringing. "Hi, is this Lisa?" the caller wanted to know. The deep voice sounded familiar, but I just couldn't place the Midwestern accent. The friendly voice was clearly someone I knew from the past. He eventually identified himself as a former mentor from my graduate MBA program. As he spoke, I quickly had images of someone changing my flat tire one cold day in Ohio and thought I had been blessed with mentors who truly care about me, especially in times of trouble. We briefly reminisced, I then shared my good news about my new teaching position, and he joyfully congratulated me.

We talked a few minutes more and ended our conversation with him, saying he would call me right back with a mutual colleagues' phone number so I could re-connect with that person as well.

Immediately, my phone rang again; I thought it was my mentor calling back with the phone number. But it wasn't, it was my mother, who said, "Lisa are you sitting down?" I knew from the tone of her voice that this was serious. She went on to say, "Your dad was just diagnosed with cancer." My heart dropped. I was leaving to teach my new class, and this would set the tone for the day. Would my father live to see my graduation from my doctoral program? Immediately feelings of imminent death and the "C" word overcame me. The word cancer sounded so deadly. I fought back the tears as I gathered my belongings to go to campus. This too shall pass, I prayed. Others had survived this deadly disease, so why not my father? I prayed to God to please hold my father in His loving arms. As I pressed down on the gas pedal in my car as I drove down the road in this busy college town, I felt a sense of relief. I could envision my parents at my graduation standing in the stadium smiling and cheering me on. I believed then that God heard my prayers, and that powerful vision allowed me to teach my first class with much excitement and enthusiasm. Those 300 students who showed up that first day were brought into the essence of a prayer where God's healing was already moving in the spirit. Finally, on graduation day, when that vision was realized and when I saw both my parents in the stadium, I thanked God for another blessing.

I thought it is well, with my soul. "It Is Well with My Soul," a popular hymn, was written by Horatio Spafford, who testified to the salvation he found in Jesus Christ through the good and the bad times. Although my parents were still here, my thoughts resonated with Spafford's lyrics because of the testament to the salvation I found in Jesus Christ through all of the good and bad times in my own life. Yes, it is well. It is well. It is well with my soul.

Key Takeaways:
- Honor your parents while they are still here.
- Problems will come and go—have faith.
- God is a Healer.

Prayer:
Lord, I am more than grateful for the relationship that I have with my earthly parents. You heavenly Father, You initiated this relationship by creating this blessed union. May this continually evolve into a beautiful legacy of love and sustenance that leads back to you. Amen.

God Watches Over Me

"The eyes of the Lord are in every place keeping watch on the evil and the good." Proverbs 15:3

"Okay, baby doll, I will drop you to the bridge, but I don't drive in the city anymore because those people drive crazy over there," my 83-year-old godfather said with a chuckle in his strong West Indian accent. "That's fine, Uncle John, " I laughed. "I can just catch the bus and subway after you drop me off, and then I will meet you back here later." As I stepped out of his new smelling car, I began my little day get-away as a "tourist" in the Big Apple. It had been years since I planned a day to just hang out in the city by myself. Graduate school was behind me, and finally, I had some free time. Oblivious to the honking horns, tourists with cameras, and multitudes of people speaking various languages, I drifted off towards the station and waited for the next train.

Since I knew the time would go by very fast, I first headed to Times Square to find something to eat. Nathan's Hotdog, A Big Warm Brown Pretzel with hot mustard, a big cheesy slice of NY Style Pizza, Sushi, or a Bagel with Tuna? Mmmm, too many choices. In reality, I really didn't care. I was simply hungry and just wanted something to fill my stomach and something to remind me of the good old days living on NYC's outskirts on the Jersey side of the bridge. The wait in line seemed like forever as I finally reached in my purse and handed my bills to the little deli's cashier. Trying to juggle my subway sandwich, the bottle of water, the snack for later, some napkins, and my purse, I thought to myself; maybe I should have sat down to eat. But I quickly remembered that I was on a schedule and on a mission to see as much as possible before I headed back to the bridge to meet my godfather. The smells of so many good foods from all over the world invading my nostrils kept me wondering if I should have kept looking. Maybe I should have ordered a full meal and taken more time peering out the deli window at all of the interesting sights on Broadway. "People Watching" in NYC was always a tourist attraction in and of itself. In the middle of my thoughts, I had an inkling to go to the Empire

State Building. I still remember when it was considered the tallest building in the world. But that was then; this was now. It no longer held that impressive distinction, but it was still a famous landmark worth visiting again. As I waited for the elevator inside the lobby of the Empire State Building, two men, one white with dirty blond hair, one Latino with a cap on, both about my age, approached the elevator to also go up to the top floor to the World Observatory. We engaged in light conversation and ironically found out that the one with the dirty blond hair had graduated high school the same year I did in the town next to mine. He came with his friend from California, and both of them, like me, also just wanted to be an NYC tourist for a day. During our brief conversation, I mentioned my desire to also visit the famous Twin Towers. They explained they had just come from over there and that it was extremely crowded with tourists. They laughed and let me know that I made the right decision by being at the Empire State Building during this time. Their comforting words would soon come back to haunt my memory in a jarring way five days later. In the meantime, however, we continued to talk about our Jersey roots and life in general until the elevator came and took the 3 of us up 110 flights to the very top. We said our good-byes and parted ways. We never saw each other again.

Succumbing to my fear of heights at the time, I glanced from a distance towards the street 110 flights down below. Then I cautiously inched toward the gated bar windows that separated us from the big white fluffy clouds in the sky. My heart skipped several beats when I opened my eyes and actually saw how high we were in the air. Despite my fear, at the moment, I took out my little yellow disposable camera and snapped a quick picture of a pigeon that came and perched on the window screen in front of me. It was a close-up shot, and I had no idea of what was lurking in the background behind this pigeon's head until I had the picture developed a few weeks later. Pleased with my moment of courage to stand 110 flights in the air, I was more than ready to catch the next elevator back down to the first floor, where my feet would be firmly planted back on the ground. Taking in a few more sights of the city, I determined in my mind that I would continue my sightseeing extravaganza sooner rather than later. If I had time, I might even come back tomorrow, I thought to myself. Back in NJ, in the condo that evening, I shared with my godfather what a nice time I had and my desire to continue my tourist journey.

He was more than happy to ask if I wanted to stay a few more days, tour the city and stay for a family cookout on the weekend. My heart said yes, but my mouth said no. I explained that I had signed a contract back in SC, and as much as I wanted to stay and hang out with family and hang out in the city, I knew I needed to go home. He pleaded for me to stay for the weekend and said, "Are you sure? I can drop you back to the bridge." But I had to say no; I had a commitment I needed to honor at 9 am Tuesday. On my long flight back home, I thought about the pigeon, the guys in the elevator, my godfather's humorous stories dating back to the 1930s, the city food, and the family cookout I was missing. These thoughts disappeared as I sat on the Navy Base's hard chair in Charleston, preparing to start our "train the trainer" session that Tuesday morning. The eight of us around the table quickly began small chit-chat discussing how we found out about the training and describing our weekend's adventures. Then someone's cell phone rang, and amid our conversations, we heard her say, "Honey, I can't talk now; the training is getting ready to start; I will call you back when we get a break." She noticed everyone had paused to look at her, and she explained, "Oh, that was just my husband saying something about a plane crash. I told him I would talk to him later." As soon as she hung up, however, he called right back. The look on her face while nervously yelling, "what happened, are you serious?" was overshadowed by the staff member at the base in full uniform bursting through the door saying, "The United States is being attacked, you must get off the base. Grab all of your things; everyone needs to leave immediately." We all seemed stunned but followed his commanding orders. We hurried out the door, grabbing our things, and frantically pulled out our cell phones to call our loved ones as we all headed towards our cars. Now the conversation we overheard from our team member and her husband made total sense. We, the US, were under some type of serious attack, and this was no joke. I just headed home, driving as if I was in a trance, wanting to make sure that my family was okay, to make sure they were safe, and to make sure they were all still alive.

Like many others in the world for the next few weeks, I was fixated on the television in the living room upon reaching home. Minute by minute, station after station, I watched in horror as the enemies' planes kept crashing into the Twin Towers. I prayed for the survivors. I prayed for the ones who lost their loved ones, and I prayed that some would emerge from the rubble by God's grace. Yet, each replay of the plane crashes seemed to be more horrific than the original broadcast. To be honest, sitting on the couch, I felt like I had an out-of-body experience. Tears fell as I watched balls of fire on the TV screen erupt in flames, bodies falling out of windows, and people covered in ash walking and running through the streets of Manhattan. I knew people who worked in the tower and the district and wondered if they could be in the rubble?

Did they just jump out of the window? I watched in horror as local, and federal investigators traced the steps of the terrorists from Newark Airport, where I flew out to get home, to downtown Manhattan, from the Empire State Building to the Twin Towers and other midtown sites. I hardly ate for a week because I was so engrossed in watching the news, what seemed like 24/7. Terrorist experts tried to track everywhere they thought the terrorists might have been in the weeks before the attack. During this drama on TV, it dawned on me that my journey was not too far off from those of the terrorists. Where they had been, I had been.

Had I not been obedient and come home to participate in this pre-scheduled "train the trainer" session, I might not be here to tell this story. Even as I sat in my living room watching these horrific replays of a major murder plot unfolding before my eyes, I was reminded of how at a moment's notice, our life can swiftly come to an end. Then weeks later, I took a moment to go through the pictures I took in NYC, hoping to gain some sense of peace and normalcy back into my life. Yet, when I came to the picture of the pigeon, I was shocked. The background behind the pigeon's head was the faint image of the two famous Twin Towers, hovering over NYC like giants in the sky. Only this time, even these tall giant buildings made out of steel tubular materials were no match for Osama Bin Laden and his al-Qaeda organization. The cowardly acts of these men and their cronies brought these giant buildings crumbling to the ground. Sadly, the heinous crimes of these terrorists resulted in almost 3,000 people being killed starting at 8:46 am that Tuesday morning. This was the same time I sat in the Charleston Naval Base training room when the husband of our teammate frantically called his wife to warn her of danger. Yes, by God's grace and mercy, I survived this deadly attack on our country, but my heart goes out to all who lost their lives in New York City, Washington, DC, and Pennsylvania on that dreadful Tuesday morning. When the hijackers flew two Boeing 767 Aircraft into the twin towers, when they flew American Airlines Flight 77 into the Pentagon and crashed United Airlines flight 93 into a barren field in Pennsylvania, they simultaneously pierced the heart of the American people. These four appalling acts sparked outrage in this country, the likes of which had never been seen before.

Through the tears, the pain, and the trauma, up from the ashes arose a nation which for a time believed that when one hurts, we all hurt. While this love for one another did not last forever, I believe it at least gave a brief glimpse of when Jesus says, "Greater love has no one than this, than to lay down one's life for his friends." People laid down their lives for their friends and co-workers, but they also laid down their lives for strangers. It was a season where people truly did show love to one another. Thinking back to this unforgettable week, I think about all that happened, the good, the bad, and the ugly. I also think about the pigeon, which I encountered 110 floors above ground, and I can't help but think that God had his hands on me guiding me all the time. For me, that pigeon symbolized a sparrow, and I recalled the lyrics so often sung in church, "When Jesus is my portion?/A constant Friend is He: His eye is on the sparrow,/And I know He watches over me."

I am convinced that God not only watched over me that entire week but guided me safely back home to my family.

Key Takeaways:
- Honor your commitments.
- Be a risk-taker, trust God.
- Know that God is guiding, protecting, and directing you and that God loves you.

Prayer:
Lord, thank you for going before me and bringing up love even out the ashes. You are a provider even in times of crisis. When we find ourselves in the darkness, you become our way maker and deliverer. For that, I am thankful, in Jesus' name, I pray. Amen.

Passion for Justice

"For I the Lord love justice, hate robbery, and wrongdoing; I will faithfully give them their recompense, and I will make an everlasting covenant with them." Isaiah 61:8

No Justice, No Peace, No Justice, No Peace. The chants got louder and louder. Then the crowd got bigger and bigger, and the heat got hotter and hotter.

Twenty Thousand people packed together in a little town called Jena.

They did not descend on this little southern town by chance. Black radio hosts from urban stations and civil rights leaders strongly encouraged people to drop what they were doing and make their way to Jena. Their passionate call across the radio waves and on social media drew hundreds and thousands to Jena, Louisiana, from across the nation and worldwide. It all started when a black high school student asked his white classmates if it was okay to sit under a tree. In response to his innocent question, a noose was hanging in the same tree the next day. This incident enraged large numbers of blacks and allies who still harbored memories of lynching, violence, and hate. Then months later, five African American students at Jena High School severely beat one of their white classmates. In turn, the prosecutor's office charged them with attempted murder. Many in the community, especially blacks, found these charges outrageous and heeded the call to show up in Jena on that fall day in September 2007. At the time, it was considered the largest civil rights demonstration in years. As a faculty member teaching about human rights and social justice, I also heeded the call. With 20 African American Student leaders, I hopped in a van and headed to Jena to support the men who came to be known as the Jena 6.

Some others came on bikes, others rode buses and trucks, some took airplanes, but we all came for one cause---to protest racial injustice, which flared up again in the good old US of A. The students and I made our way through the crowd. We tried to get as close to the main speakers as possible. As their faculty advisor, I had to keep my eyes on the group and them. I was not worried about the students getting into trouble, but tensions were high surrounding this national cause, and anything was possible. The local news station in Charleston, SC chronicled our trip on the evening news the day we boarded the van to leave town. Why were we going, and what did we hope to accomplish they wanted to know? As the beads of sweat dripped down my cheeks, I was still trying to come up with an answer to the reporter's question. Answering this question was no easy feat. We crammed together like sardines packed in a can. At one point, the heat was so intense that I felt nauseous and weak. I thought I was going to pass out, but thankfully I didn't.

During the 24 hours in town, we witnessed nothing but peaceful protestors, camaraderie among strangers, and a passion for justice that echoed throughout the community. We came seeking answers to the age-old question that has plagued this country for years. Why does having black skin seem to draw so much hatred from others in our country? We left Jena still pondering this question but having a greater understanding of how deeply rooted systemic oppression brings out the best and the worst of people. We also left Jena knowing that this wasn't merely a Jena problem but a global one. W.E.B Dubois, a Civil Rights Activist and the first African American to graduate from Harvard, said it best when he wrote, "The issue of the twentieth century is the problem of the color line. Dubois made this comment based on racial issues he witnessed around the world. Unfortunately, this was now the twenty-first century, and Dr. Dubois' words were hauntingly still ringing true.

Key Takeaways:
- Love your neighbor and Love Justice.
- Love always overcomes hate.
- Your enemies may hurt you but love them anyhow.

Prayer
Sustainer, Deliverer, Redeemer, I am grateful for your holy presence in a world that straddles between love and hate. May you surround me with Angels that bring comfort in times of trouble. Lord, bless me and keep me as I meditate on your goodness. In the precious name of Jesus. Amen.

Anger in the Valley

"Put away from you all bitterness and wrath and anger and wrangling and slander, together with all malice, and be kind to one another, tenderhearted, forgiving one another, as God in Christ has forgiven you."
Ephesians 4:31-32

Several years ago, I met a young woman named Arianna in her early 30's. She explained that her teenager got seriously injured in a hit-and-run accident the night before we met. She was devastated. That afternoon I accompanied her to the hospital to see her daughter, who suffered severe injuries, including several broken bones and fractures.

The doctors eventually informed Arianna that Simone, her "baby," would be partially paralyzed for life and possibly never walk again. Upon hearing this news and seeing her child lying in a hospital bed with bandages and tubes all over her body, Arianna expressed that she was angry, scared, depressed, and confused. She wanted to strike out at the doctors, God, and anybody else in her path.

She mainly wanted to lash out at the unidentified person who left her daughter for dead and almost hit her two young "beautiful" toddlers. For the next few weeks, I was there as a sounding board, a confidant, a caregiver, and a prayer partner.

The night after the accident, I took her two children to my family home and agreed to watch them over the next few days while she took care of urgent legal and medical issues with the police and hospital.

Since it was a hit-and-run accident and near the Christmas holidays, the media ran an article about the incident. The media attention allowed Arianna to see that the community did care about what happened. It resulted in many viewers sending her prayers, holiday gifts for the children, and cash donations to help with expenses. It also paved the way for others to come forward to help take care of the children on a long-term basis until Arianna could get back on her feet.

Thus, I believe that God put me in Arianna's life at that particular time to give her space to vent her true feelings and to allow her to see that God can still work miracles. While Simone did lose use of her leg, she was released from the hospital to be with her family. At times, I offered Arianna silence as she cried, vented, or cursed whoever was her target for that day. It was a very horrific experience, but I prayed to God to provide me with the right words to say to someone who was hurting so deeply.

For the most part, I believe that my presence was effective and came across as caring, calming, and helpful. But sometimes, I wondered if I could have said more to help Arianna deal with all the raw feelings she had from this experience.

Since she didn't know the identity of the driver who hit her child, I silently wondered would she ever be at peace.

What if her teenager never walked again? Could she find it in her heart to thank the doctors for at least providing Simone the medical care that they did? Will Arianna ever reconcile with God? These are the questions that still linger in my mind. I kept in touch with her for about a year but found out that she relocated sometime later. The reality is that I may never see her again to find out the answers to these questions. I pray and hope that my approach to this helping incident provided a confidential and caring space for a mother with such deep pain.

During our time together, I tried to impart to Arianna that God is loving, compassionate, and merciful. I also wanted to assure her that there is a space for lament in our lives. I shared with her Psalm 13, Jeremiah's crying, "...How long wilt thou hide thy face from me? How long must I bear pain in my soul and have sorrow in my heart all the day?" I also encouraged her to seek and thank God by praying the words of Psalm 23, "Yea, though I walk through the valley of the shadow of death, I will fear no evil; for thou art with me; thy rod and thy staff, they comfort me." I intended to show Arianna that suffering is just a part of our spiritual journey but that God will be there in the midst of our suffering. I pray that at least some of my message resonated with this young, dedicated mother.

Key Takeaways:
- Your pain is never too harsh for God to handle.
- It's okay to vent but release your frustration and turn it over to God.
- Open your heart to others whom God has placed in Your Life.

Prayer

Oh God, our Father, I come to you today with my pent-up frustrations and anger. Help me to release these feelings to you. Help me to channel situations I can't control into your Glory. Remove me out of the way so you can guide me and direct me and fill me with a peace that transcends all understanding. Through Jesus Christ, I pray. Amen.

God Has Prepared A Place

"In my Father's house, there are many dwelling places. If it were not so, would I have told you that I go to prepare a place for you?" John 14:2

The coming of Easter Sunday growing up illuminated memories of sunny picture-perfect weather for making Easter Baskets stuffed with light green straw grass, various chocolates and candies, little toys, and painted eggs. This particular Easter, however, was far from those glorious memories. The weather forecaster predicted that there would be rain and lots of it. The thunderstorms that drenched the Low Country that week brought with it torrential rains, heavy, gusty winds, and dangerous streaks of lightning.

This Easter weekend was neither a time for little girls to wear pretty frilly dresses in the park nor the time for searching for colorful eggs in the local church cemetery. As I listened to the rain pitter-patter on my roof, I had an eerie feeling in my gut that something wasn't right, but I just couldn't put my finger on it. In reflection, this probably should have been a sign that something was amiss on the other side of town, but I just attributed it to all the bad weather coming down outside my window.

It wasn't until several days later that I found out that this treacherous storm caused a huge tree to fall through "Ms. Jackson's" roof. A close family friend of my parents, I felt compelled to see how she was doing. Upon seeing the damage for myself and offering Ms. J some help, I gasped when she opened the door. It looked like a scene that someone staged for a horror movie. The dangling particles of tree branches, mosquitoes, gnats, and other flying bugs mixed in with electrical wires and rainwater on the floor and scattered throughout Ms. J's bedroom now looked like a warzone. The mildew smell emanating from the wet clothes and bedding didn't help make the scene more bearable. I had to step back to take a breath of fresh air.

"Are you okay?" I asked Ms. J. Teary-eyed, she explained that she religiously goes to bed every night after watching the 10:00 pm nightly news. This night she said that God told her, "don't go to bed yet." She remarked that she was so thankful for listening to God because it was 10:00 pm when the giant tree came crashing down through the roof of her modest trailer and landed over her bed. I can tell she was grateful to God, but she was also clearly still terrified about almost possibly losing her life or at the very least suffering bodily damage.

A couple of days later, Cassie, the young reporter, and her videographer Bryan pulled into the driveway just as I watched Ms. J wipe the tears from her eyes. The sounds of the big wheels on the SUV grinding over the dirt and pebbles lining the driveway brought our conversation to a standstill. The young blond reporter gleefully hopped out of the vehicle and walked towards us with a warm smile. She kindly introduced herself and relayed her purpose for her visit. She wanted to know the details of the large tree that fell through Ms. J's house. Moreover, she wanted to know the details behind the story of the infamous tree that was circulating town. City officials said there wasn't a story, just a private resident who had a slight misfortune.

Ms. J's teary eyes and solemn look told another story. Her home was a private residence, but this was no slight misfortune. For a moment, there was a gulf of silence. Cassie, holding her portable microphone, looked at Ms. J and Ms. J looked at the young reporter. Bryan, carrying his video equipment, and I stared at them, staring at each other. It seemed like a sacred moment where silent truth became more important than the spoken word. With her reporter instincts, Cassie quickly turned her gaze away from Ms. J's eyes and turned towards Ms. J's house and motioned for Bryan to follow her.

She asked Ms. J if it was okay to go inside, and Ms. J, in a quiet voice, responded yes. As soon as Cassie opened the door, she yelled, "Oh My God, the tree is still here." Bryan, with his camera, ran to see what caused Cassie to react the way she did. The startled look on his face said it all. The remnants of the tree were still there. The wires, the electrical cords, the debris, the gnats, the mosquitoes, and the wet wood were all there dripping over her mildew-smelling bedding and clothes. The city could not deny the story circulating town. The evidence was hanging right in front of Cassie and Bryan. They had no choice but to air what they witnessed that day on the local nightly news. When the story did air, the community members were shocked.

The City Officials had explaining to do because their explanation of a minor occurrence was no laughing matter. Ms. J worked all her life in NYC then retired in Charleston County. She was relieved that the news finally told her story. The city agreed to assist Ms. J with getting a newer trailer. She was heartbroken and shaken by the whole ordeal but grateful that she would soon have a new home. Unfortunately, she died of medical complications before the trailer was ready to be occupied. Some of her close friends said it was the result of this ordeal that killed her. At her funeral, I had the honor and privilege to remind those in attendance that Ms. J was a fighter, a trailblazer, and a woman who loved the Lord. I relayed that she would never sleep in the home provided by the city. In the end, however, I truly believed that God had already prepared a place for Ms. J to go. She would go to a new home where there would be no more pain, no more sorrow, and no more tears. This heavenly home would be a place with her Savior, one she could truly call home.

GOD HAS PREPARED A PLACE

Key Takeaways:
- Storms in life can come at a moment's notice-but God is still there.
- God has already prepared a place to call home where there will be no suffering, no pain, and no sorrow.
- God wants us to look after, care for and help the widows in our community.

Prayer:
Eternal and Merciful God, we commit all widows into your loving hands, and may you care for them according to Your Word. Equip me, O God, to humble myself and care for them as you care for me. And may you heal the brokenhearted and bind up their wounds even in a storm. Thank you in the name of Jesus. Amen and Amen.

Lord, I Look to You

"The Lord went in front of them in a pillar of cloud by day, to lead them along the way, and in a pillar of fire by night, to give them light, so that they might travel by day and by night." Exodus 13:21

Jacket, airline ticket, passport, visa, money—check. Bible, books to read, and my gospel CD with 10 hours' worth of my gospel favorites, which I had my cousin download before I left for the airport—check. Everything I needed was here, and at least my CD would get me through a third of the trip. Earlier in the week, the local newspaper ran a story about my upcoming mission trip to South Africa to minister to Women and Children living with HIV and AIDS. Now the day had finally arrived. Waiting in line to get my boarding pass, I made mental notes of the busy terminal. The remembrance of September 11, 2001 still keeps my radar on guard when I am near an airport. And so, I watched couples pushing strollers with small children, a skycap pushing an older woman in a wheelchair, teenagers sporting their soccer team jerseys, and police officers with their police dogs, watching and pacing the floor. The airport seemed busier than usual today. I hope there is no unexpected delay with taking off. My driver will meet me in Johannesburg (Joburg) at 2 pm the next day. I pulled out the little slip of paper where I jotted his name and number down—Mbuso, +2711 343-0202.

I didn't want to lose this piece of paper because Mbuso came highly recommended, and I didn't want to find myself stranded in Joburg. My memories from my first trip to South Africa fifteen years prior were a stark reminder to have fun and be safe, especially as a female traveling alone. I pushed the paper back into my purse, and then the baggage announcements began. "Please do not leave your luggage unattended. Unattended luggage may be removed or destroyed by the security services. Please keep your baggage with you at all times." "With all the crime and crazy stuff going on in this world, especially at airports, why would someone leave the luggage unattended?", I said to myself. Minutes later, I finally made it through security and onto the plane. Placing my small suitcase in the overhead above me, I could now slink down in my seat and prepare for take-off. This flight would be a long one, but I hoped for a peaceful ride to the motherland. Before I could sit down in my assigned middle seat, I heard someone say, "Hi, I think I'm in that seat," pointing to the vacant seat next to me. He was a tall gentleman with a strong Southern dialect. "Hi," I replied, "Is Joburg your final destination too?" I asked him? "Yes," he said, "I am heading there for a brief business trip and taking in some of the sights. How about you?" "I'm going over to do ministry and also to take in some of the sights as well," I responded. After settling in my seat and a couple of minutes of small talk, the announcements began. I began listening to the attendant with the Swedish accent. Still, due to a brief stint working for the airlines years ago, I found myself, like many others reciting the lines in my head, half-listening as the attendant's voice came over the speaker system. "Good evening, ladies and gentlemen. Welcome aboard Delta flight 9899 to Frankfurt with continuing service to Johannesburg. Thank you for your attention while important safety information is reviewed. In preparation for departure, be certain that your seat back is straight up and your tray table is stowed. Make sure that your carry-on items are placed completely under the seat in front of you."[i] As soon as we were allowed to use our own devices, I quickly put my earplugs in and turned on my gospel CD. I began listening to Break Every Chain, Nobody Greater, and then "YES" by Shekinah Glory. We were so high up in the clouds, for a few minutes, I thought I was in heaven.

"Ma'am, would you like something to eat?" the friendly flight attendant asked. I didn't realize I had fallen asleep that fast. I was more tired than I wanted to admit. Getting to the airport without much sleep the day before began to take a toll. "Ma'am, would you like something to eat, the friendly flight attendant asked again?" As my stomach growled, I said, "Yes," and put my tray down to eat. Afterward, I listened to my gospel tracks again, watched a couple of movies, woke up to eat, and fell asleep several times until we finally landed in South Africa.

Excited and tired, I waited patiently around the carrousel to collect my luggage. Ignoring all of the announcements above, I waited for what seemed like hours. By now, the crowd had thinned out, and most people I recognized from my flight had left the baggage area. The passengers left a few bags at the turnstile; then I thought I heard the announcement say, "Robinson come to the office." Is that my imagination, or did they say, Robinson? I wasn't sure because of the African dialect. I didn't want to leave the baggage carousel if my big suitcase was coming, but then I thought it might be Mbuso coming to pick me up. I didn't want him to think I hadn't arrived. I also hadn't exchanged my money yet and didn't want to go through that hassle right now to get a cab to take me to the center for Women and Children, where I would be staying. Just to be sure, I dragged my small red suitcase to the office, and the clerk immediately looked at me and said "Robinson?" with a heavy accent.

"Did you say, Robinson?" I asked him.

"Yes, did you just come from Atlanta?" he asked.

"Yes, I did," still thinking he just wanted to let me know my ride was here.

"Can I see your ticket?" he asked. I showed it to him, and he informed me that my large suitcase with all of my clothes, toiletries, papers, and other essential documents was still sitting in Atlanta at the airport. Quickly apologizing for the airline, he said he could get me a $50 voucher to buy some clothes to hold me until my bag arrived, hopefully in the next couple of days. "Please keep your baggage with you at all times," is what I recalled the announcer warned all passengers. I looked down at my little suitcase with two days worth of clothes and thought, thank you, God, for giving me what I need to get me by for a few days. All of those Gospel songs started reverberating in my mind.

Kirk Franklin's 'Smile,' Smokie Norful's 'I Need You Now' and Whitney Houston's 'I look to You' allowed me to take in what the clerk was saying and not fret about it. I also found comfort in remembering,"…we know that all things work together for good to them that love God, to them who are called according to his purpose." Things could be worse, I thought. He got me a voucher, and I thanked him. I connected with Mbuso, the driver, a few minutes later, standing in the taxi area holding up a sign up with my name. We greeted each other and headed in his van to the center on the outskirts of town. I knew deep down in my heart that this would be the beginning of a very eventful trip.

Key Takeaways:
- You don't need to carry a lot of baggage.
- Fill your mind with the Word.
- God has already provided.

Prayer
Eternal and Gracious God, I need you right now. Help me remember that all things work together for good for those who love the Lord and are called according to His purpose. Remind me, O God, even when things go wrong, to be grateful for the blessings I have before me. Lord, I thank you from the bottom of my heart for your faithfulness. It is in your name that I sing these praises. Amen.

Make Room at Your Banquet

"But when you give a banquet, invite the poor, the crippled, the lame, and the blind. And you will be blessed because they cannot repay you, for you will be repaid at the resurrection of the righteous." Luke 14:13-14

"Thambo, can you please come to give me a hand in the kitchen? Ms. Lisa has a flight to catch, and we want to eat lunch before we take her to the airport," she called from the kitchen. "Ok, ma'am, I'm coming. Ms. Lisa, are you hungry?" "Yes, I am," I gladly replied to Thambo, impressed by the affection and polite mannerism naturally displayed by this bright-eyed, delightful eight-year-old. As he ran off to the kitchen, my eyes became fixated on the life-size picture hanging on their living room wall. The massive painting in the quaint living room was of Thambo's big brother and Gail's adopted son, Nkosi Johnson.

They both said that Nkosi was their hero. As Thambo made his way to the kitchen, I realized that his proper diction and mannerisms were eerily familiar to his brother, even though I had never met Nkosi in person. I only knew him by what I saw and heard on the internet and through my conversations with Gail. By the time I even knew who Nkosi was, he was already deceased. But it was because of Nkosi that I was once again visiting South Africa. I found his life story to be fascinating and inspiring. Even South African President Nelson Mandela, who invited Nkosi to his house, was moved by Nkosi's honesty and caring spirit, just as millions of others who either met him in person or who heard him speak at the International World's Aid conference. Nkosi's interaction with President Mandela brought a smile to my face because we went to President Mandela's house in Pretoria on my first trip to South Africa. The guard told my sister, cousin, and friends from Joburg at the front gate that "the old man was sleeping." We were told later on by many locals that had we said we were visiting from America, that President Mandela would have gladly come to greet us. We wish we would have known that then. Well, at least Nkosi got to meet him in person. Nkosi was the longest-surviving child with HIV in South Africa who used his plight in life to help create

"Nkosi's Haven," a place of comfort for women and children living with HIV or AIDS.

Sadly, Nkosi succumbed to the full-blown AIDs virus before he could fully witness his dream come true. My time at Nkosi's Haven praying with the mothers, playing and tutoring the children, cooking in the kitchen, and helping in the brand-new bakery was a blessing in itself. As Thambo brought my lunch plate to me with a smile, he said, "Ms. Lisa, I have your lunch." I graciously thanked him, and I could see Nkosi's loving spirit operating inside of his younger brother. I could also see how the love Gail shared with Nkosi and Thambo extended to the community of children and mothers living at Nkosi's Haven, some with the virus and some not, some orphaned, some not. These mothers and children still had joy and laughter, even amid their suffering and discrimination. The twelve big boxes of toiletries, clothes, books, prayer blankets, toys, and household supplies that I collected from caring individuals in the US were welcomed with open arms and were more than appreciated.

Moreover, the 13th International Aids conference broadcast Nkosi's words to millions of people around the world. He contracted the virus from his HIV-positive mother while she was pregnant. Gail, who is white and was a volunteer at the center where Nkosi and his mother stayed, took him in when his dying mom could no longer care for him. This bond was the beginning of the special relationship between Gail and Nkosi, as mother and son. It was not easy as people hurled stereotypes and discrimination at them. Yet, the petite 12-year-old Nkosi captured the hearts of many at the televised convention by simply saying, "Care for us and accept us — we are all human beings. We are normal. We have hands. We have feet. We can walk, we can talk, we have needs just like everyone else. Don't be afraid of us. We are all the same!"[ii]

This small 12-year-old with the big heart de-stigmatized how people treated others with HIV and AIDs Worldwide. In Zulu, the name Nkosi means Lord or King or Chief. With such a short life span, God used this young King to challenge discriminatory practices in South Africa and worldwide. In his unique way, he was telling the world that discriminating against others was wrong and hurtful. In other words, if you were planning a banquet, make sure to invite the orphans, the children with HIV and Aids, and the poor, those who Jesus would call the "least of these." Nkosi gave a powerful message that people heard near and far and he was the perfect one to deliver it. As a result, in 2005, Gail, on Nkosi's behalf, received the International Children's Peace Prize, a prestigious award given annually to a child who made significant contributions advocating children's rights and improving the situation of vulnerable children such as orphans, child laborers and Children with HIV/AIDS. Even in death, Nkosi's dream lives on, and I was blessed to personally witness how his legacy is still warming the hearts of others.

Upon returning home to the US, from South Africa, I was so tired from jet lag that I crashed at my parents' house and fell asleep in one of the spare bedrooms. I was just too weary of driving the extra ten minutes to my own home. On the next day, January 12th, 2010, I woke up to loud screaming and commotion coming from the television. What I saw on the screen was utter chaos. I honestly thought I was having a nightmare. After fully waking up, I recognized that what I witnessed on the television screen was a massive 7.0 earthquake which devastated Haiti, the poorest country in the Western hemisphere. I was still sleepy from jet lag from my flight the night before, but these horrible scenes quickly brought me back to reality. The reporters estimated that the earthquake injured

300,000 people, killed 250,000, and forced 1.5 million to live in makeshift housing for the foreseeable future. This developing country was pretty much in ruins. I cried and prayed for God to work a mighty miracle for the thousands who this tragedy had impacted. My mind reverted to the September 11th deadly attacks on America in 2001 as first responders pulled dead bodies from the rubble. Then I quickly realized that God did it again.

A local missionary invited me to go with her to Port Au Prince, Haiti, before my South Africa trip. I prayed about this new opportunity, which sounded so exciting. However, I told her that I couldn't go because I had committed to going to South Africa at about the same time. I further explained that as much as I wanted to go minister to the mothers and children with HIV or AIDs at the orphanage in Haiti, I needed to honor the commitment I made previously to the mothers and children in South Africa. I promised her that I would make plans to go on one of their future trips. God truly had a hand in this situation. Had I canceled my plans for South Africa to go to Haiti instead, I too might be in the rubble dead or clinging for my life. Saddened and heartbroken by all of the lives lost in Haiti, I'm so thankful for keeping my commitment to my sisters and brothers in Johannesburg and for serving a loving God. God obviously had more Kingdom work for me to do. So, to God be all the Glory.

Key Takeaways:
- Jesus loves his children, the lame, the marginalized, and the poor.
- Words can lift you, and words can tear you down.
- Speak up when you see someone oppressing someone else.

Prayer:
Almighty God, creator of all things, we are grateful to you and seek your heavenly wisdom. Open our hearts to love those who society has deemed unworthy, including the children, the lame, and those afflicted with disease. May you show us the way to dwell together in peace and harmony. With you, we know that all things are possible. In Jesus' name, we pray. Amen.

Our Hope is in Christ

"Let us hold fast to the confession of our hope without wavering, for he who has promised is faithful."
Hebrews 10:23

"We, therefore, commit his/her body to the ground/its final resting-place; earth to earth, ashes to ashes, dust to dust. In the hope of resurrection unto eternal life, through the promise of Our Lord Jesus Christ, we faithfully and victoriously give him/her over to your blessed care. Amen."[iii]

These words rolled off my tongue as my sandals slowly pressed down into the soft red clay dirt in the cemetery. The Ghanaian heat of the sun beat down on us as we prepared for the final committal. Each Minister recited the exact words, "Earth to Earth, Ashes to Ashes...". I watched as those who gathered stared into the open graves, some wailing in pain, some clinging to loved ones, some holding private conversations on the side, others just looking solemn.

The drums in the background vibrated with an energetic African Beat. "The beat is a connection to the ancestors," my Pastor whispered in my ear. I noticed what seemed like sadness as one of the wives wiped away her tears. Preaching the funeral service with six caskets in front of me had never crossed my mind. Friends, family, and dignitaries packed the church pews. My seminary training back in the US at Princeton Seminary prepared us to do funerals in the future but not six at one time. But this was the custom in Ghana, West Africa, and I just happened to be the one chosen to eulogize the last funeral for the summer. Anybody who died after this weekend, their family would have to hold the funeral in another city or preserve their body until the Fall season, using the ancient wisdom of our foremothers and forefathers. But today, six bodies neatly arranged in six individual caskets were lined up across the front of the church in front of me, waiting for my words of comfort. What could I say? Each of the deceased had their journey on Earth, and it was my job to honor each of them respectfully. Delivery of the words of comfort was both an honor and a privilege, and I prayed that I would be up to the task. I prayed that God would use me as a vessel. As I preached the Eulogy, I peered into the pews and reminded those gathered that we all have an ending date, but our hope is in Christ. Standing in the narrow upper pulpit, fifteen feet above the six caskets on the lower level, I hoped that the message I gave translated into words of comfort for those who were grieving. My assigned translator did not disappoint me. Whatever I preached, the Young Ghanaian Minister translated with just as much passion in his strong Ghanaian dialect. This service was important because funerals in Ghana are a vital and sacred ritual. Hundreds and sometimes thousands may show up depending on who died. Dressed in a headwrap, top, and skirt with the traditional red and black funeral attire of Ghana, I began by greeting those in the pew with "Akwaaba Mema wo akwaaba" meaning "I welcome You" in the local Twi language. I watched as heads nodded in response to the words of comfort drawn from the Word of God. I listened to the joyous sounds coming from the instruments and the choir throughout the various parts of the service and swayed with the hand-clapping, foot-stomping, and dancing. It was a funeral but, it was also a Celebration of Life, and I knew that the Spirit of God was present. Tomorrow was another day, the day we would go to each deceased's home and read their last will, their

OUR HOPE IS IN CHRIST

final wishes. This ritual called the family Aiyasetenas would be another long day. "Indeed," I prayed, the Lord would make a way and once again provide me with the right words to say to the grieving families.

Key Takeaways:
- God will strengthen you and help you.
- Do not let your heart be troubled.
- God comforts those who mourn.

Prayer:
Merciful God, I pray to you for your never-ending sweet presence. Your words say we are born in your image but will return to the earth. While I am still here on Earth, may you hear my prayers for joy, hope, peace, and love. For my hope is in Christ. Amen.

The Lord Hears the Cries of the Poor

"If a brother or sister is naked and lacks daily food, and one of you says to them, "Go in peace; keep warm and eat your fill," and yet you do not supply their bodily needs, what is the good of that?" James 2:15-16

"Help Me. Help Me", she whispered with a soft utterance in her voice and deep dark-set eyes. As I walked home from the store, clutching my leftover biryani rice and roti, shivering in the cool weather, up in the Kalani Hills of Southern India, 7000 feet above sea level, I couldn't help but notice the shadow of a soul crouched down and nestled in the sidewalk. I was halfway across the world from my warm heated apartment in Princeton, NJ, standing before somebody's daughter and possibly mother or grandmother. But this was my new home, at least for the next year, a year of ministry, a year of mission work, and a year to find my role in God's plan for my life. As I stood there, I was thinking, "There but for the Grace of God, there go I." As she lifted her wrinkled and mud-covered hands toward me, for a split second, a deafening silence fell. The cars beeping their horns, the stray smelly straggly dogs sniffing for crumbs on the street, and the other strangers on the sidewalk seemed to vanish in the blink of an eye.

This travesty couldn't be happening in a world filled with wealth and resources. But it was happening. In those minute seconds, my blood ran cold, my heart began to flutter, and my emotions started to boil with partial frustration and partial compassion.

I felt frustrated from teaching women's studies and social justice for almost ten years, recalling others treating women and people of color and poor people as second-class citizens. Despite this history, I imparted to my students to help a sister or brother out if they encountered someone in trouble. Before me, my sister sat on the cold, wet cement, shivering and being passed by as if she didn't even exist. Even the dogs seemed to dismiss her, licking the dirty, moist crumbs from near her feet. Eventually, our eyes locked, and my brief moment of silence ended. I responded by placing the change I had in my hand into her hand and prayed a silent prayer. I could only think to myself, "God, Oh

God, you said you would never leave us nor forsake us. In your Word, God, you remind us that you are our comforter in times of trouble. You commanded us to look out for the poor, as they will always be among us. Comfort my sister."

Despite our geographical locations, sisters worldwide are finding themselves feeling dismissed, isolated, and devalued. You, too, may think that God has forgotten you. You, also, may feel that God has overlooked and dismissed your struggles. But we are our sister's keepers. God is no respecter of persons. God is not concerned with our skin color, the value of our possessions, or the perceived power we possess. What God is concerned with is that we love one another. God is concerned that we look out for the least of these, for this is pleasing in God's eyes. What will it profit if we don't?

Key Takeaways:
- God was there on the sidewalk too.
- God will send Angels to somehow make a way in God's time.
- It is not always easy, but we have to be open to the will of God.

Prayer:
Eternal and Everlasting God, we are comforted to know that you will never leave us nor forsake us. O God, we pray for provisions for those who are in need. We thank you for allowing us to intercede for those who are hungry, naked, or needy. May we be used as vessels to bring you honor and glory. In Jesus' name, we pray. Amen.

When God Sends Angels

"I am going to send an angel in front of you to guard you on the way and to bring you to the place that I have prepared." Exodus 23:20

It was late morning, but we finally made it to Atlanta. South Carolina's traffic was safer than the current gridlock in Atlanta, wildly weaving in and around the 1-75 loop. I had heard that many people never make it home safely on this road, and after witnessing it for myself, I could see why. Several near-accidents seemed to happen at a moment's notice. The exit for my stop was like a dream come true. As I veered off down the exit ramp behind several other cars, I slightly exhaled a breath of relief. Now I could refocus on my mission for that morning. I anticipated this to be a quick meeting with the school to get Laci registered as an incoming high school student. In my mind, this shouldn't take long. I figured they would ask a few questions, flip through her middle school file, and process all her transfer papers and medical reports from Massachusetts. Well, I was wrong.

This prestigious suburban high school sitting high up on the hill looked innocent enough as we walked into the main office. The secretary was friendly, ushered us into a waiting area, and assured us that the principal would meet with us shortly. After patiently waiting almost an hour, the principal appeared. We spoke briefly, and then he began making comments in a condescending and highly dismissive manner. On the one hand, I was right. He did flip through her file as I had anticipated. However, as soon as he finished flipping through the file, he asked me to sign on the line. When I questioned what I was signing and why he wanted me to sign something we hadn't discussed, he "professionally" explained that since she was presenting with a disability that I should sign so she could graduate with a certificate of attendance. I asked him to repeat what he stated and to clarify what he meant. He gladly repeated it without hesitation. In other words, he made it clear that by signing this paper as she entered 9th grade, she would not receive an actual diploma but rather a piece of paper saying that she legally attended school for four years.

He was very matter of fact as it was clear he had asked many parents to do this, apparently with many never questioning his demands. My instincts told me that the decorative sign perfectly placed on the wall above his head, which stated "Principal of the Year," may have played a role in intimidating many parents. Yet, I was not one of those parents. I immediately told him that I would not be signing such a paper because to do so would rob my daughter of future opportunities for college, military, or a host of other options that might happen after her high school graduation. He seemed perplexed that I had challenged his authority. I demanded to know how many other African American mothers had he conned into signing their child's future away at 14 years old.

I questioned who gave him the authority to punish African American children or any other children because God created them with differently abled bodies and minds? I demanded to know how many times he did not fully explain to parents what they were signing before they signed? Moreover, I questioned if the community understood how he was fudging his high rankings in the school district by intentionally not including the scores of students who may not be high achievers. When I left, the look of embarrassment on his face, which had turned red, made it clear to me that I had exposed an ongoing system of inequality in the Atlanta suburbs.

As I departed the school, I was clear that this was not an isolated case, but it was one battle that I could not take on, at least not at the moment. For now, I was able to save my daughter, but I dread to think how many other uninformed parents were unknowingly signing their children's educational lives away. Having received my Doctorate in Social Justice Education a few weeks prior, I was more than astute to know that this behavior plays a significant role in the school-to-prison pipeline. This ordeal led me to redirect my efforts back to enroll her in school in South Carolina. Moving to the ATL would have to wait for another time. A few days after this incident, my brother ironically connected with the same 'principal of the year' at soccer practice.

Both of their sons played in the same soccer league. I am not sure how he knew that was my brother. However, my brother reported that he said, "your sister sure is tough." I interpreted his comment to mean that he knew he asked the wrong mother to sign his papers. Hopefully, he understands the seriousness of his actions before asking another family to sign on the line.

Despite the deplorable act by this principle, there was a sweet spot in all of this. A few days before relocating back to South Carolina, my sister-in-law invited a friend to dinner. She specifically asked her to come over because she had a five-year-old son who also had been diagnosed with hydrocephalus like Laci.

As a mother who already experienced a lot with the medical and school systems, my sister-in-law hoped that I could offer her friend some advice and words of encouragement for her son. We ended up having a nice dinner, and as Sheree was leaving, she said to Devon, her very active five-year-old, "let's get ready to go because you have an appointment with Dr. Greenbriar tomorrow morning to check your shunt." I couldn't believe my ears. Dr. Greenbriar was the same name as the neurosurgeon who had performed Laci's brain surgery when she was three days old in Ohio. Could it be the same doctor? What was the chance of that? To put any doubts aside, I called the number Sheree gave me the very next morning. Amazingly, it was the same doctor. He explained that he did work at the hospital where Laci was born but left Ohio years ago and then relocated to Atlanta. After a brief and very cordial conversation, Dr. Greenbriar highly encouraged us to have Laci checked by neurosurgeons when we got back to South Carolina just as a precaution to make sure everything was fine. This revelation all had to be God-ordained. When the doctors in Charleston checked Laci, they found that her shunt had come apart and she needed emergency surgery.

Upon hearing this news, we thanked God for my sister-in-law for arranging this last-minute dinner. We thanked God for Devon's mother mentioning Dr. Steven Greenbriar's name, and we thanked God for Dr. Greenbriar encouraging us to get Laci checked in Charleston. Finally, we thanked God for the Charleston doctors who performed the surgery professionally and timely. In reflection, I realized that Laci was never supposed to go to school in Atlanta, and we weren't supposed to live in Atlanta. The encounter with that "principal of the year" and Devon's mom was just an emergency layover orchestrated by God, which I have no doubt ultimately saved Laci's life. What would have happened if the doctor didn't lead us to have her shunt checked? What might have happened if we weren't obedient to God's Word. The Bible says, "My sheep listen to my voice; I know them, and they follow me." Thank God we were attuned to God's voice during our time in Atlanta.

Key Takeaways:
- Some encounters are lessons to bless you.
- Know your worth-don't just sign your life away- You are a child of God, and you are the head and not the tail.
- God strategically places some people to help you.

Prayer:
Gracious and Loving God, thank you that you never leave us alone. Thank you that Your Grace is sufficient. Remind me to listen for your voice amid all the societal noise. May you continue to surround me with angels. Through Jesus Christ Our Lord. Amen.

Don't Pass Me By

"Happy are those who consider the poor; the Lord delivers them in the day of trouble." Psalm 41:1

It was freezing outside. This holiday season was one of the last Christmas breaks my twin sister Lori and I would have before graduating college. We watched the fluffy white snowdrops, which had already turned to brown slush, splatter under each car's tires that drove by us. During the holidays, coming to NYC was always a treat, especially seeing the streets lit up in bright festive Christmas colors. We walked hurriedly to get to the streetlamp on the corner. Across the road, St. Luke's Hospital stood on the corner, overshadowing the long Manhattan block. We were there to see my Aunt Flo, who the hospital admitted the other day. Cars went by on the slushy roads, but not many people were out on this winter evening. They were probably home snuggled up near their fireplace. Others were perhaps already tucked into bed.

Still, others wished they had a warm place to snuggle. We shivered as we made it to the corner. A few seconds later, we glanced behind us to see our parents still locking the car doors and getting their belongings from the trunk. Standing not far from us was an older man who appeared homeless. We could see the layers of tattered old newspapers protruding from under his torn brown jacket. As we passed him, he smiled and said "hi" and slowly continued down the street. We said "hello" as we had always spoken to strangers and welcomed them as we would welcome anybody else. As we waited for our parents, we looked back and noticed that they were now talking to the same man we had just spoken to on the corner. We assumed they were saying hi and would begin walking towards us to cross the street and visit our aunt in the hospital. But they both began to motion to us, waving their hands to tell us to come to them. We obliged and wondered what was going on. Was this man in trouble? Were they trying to help him, we wondered?

Well, we soon found out that this "homeless" man was our uncle. He was our father's brother whom we hadn't seen in years. He was waiting outside the hospital to see the same Aunt we came to visit because that was also his sister. He had survived walking the city streets for 40 years. I thought, unlike the Israelites who were wandering, he knew exactly where he was and what he was doing. We were amazed when he opened his long-tattered coat and pulled out an old accordion plastic roll of pictures, including pictures of us when we were babies. He also had pictures of our brothers, Vernon and Derek, Uncle Lewis, and many cousins, aunts, and uncles. He had photos of the whole family under his torn coat. Today wasn't exactly the warmest day to be having a family reunion on the streets of Manhattan. Yet, we were glad that we honored our upbringing by speaking to someone who knew us before we even knew us. What if we had passed him by without saying anything? What if our parents weren't there? We may have never known he was a blood relative. We also may not have known that Jesus' teaching on the least of us hit so close to home.

Key Takeaways:
- Be kind to the poor.
- Treat the homeless with respect.
- Speak to and acknowledge those less fortunate; don't just pass by them.

Prayer:

Precious Holy Spirit remind us to keep our hearts open to those who may be poor or homeless. May you guide us to listen to them and share the Word of God and whatever resources we have to help sustain them. We pray that you provide them with warmth and peace as you bless us with a caring spirit to love. In Jesus' Name, we pray. Amen.

Death Still Has No Sting

"Where, O death, is your victory? Where, O death, is your sting?" 1 Corinthians 15:55

"Where's Sharon with the potato salad? She's not here yet; Sharon is on the subway coming from Brooklyn," someone retorted, with Marvin Gaye's 'What's Going On' blaring from the portable boom box in the back of the bus. "Sharon should have been here already. She knew what time we were leaving," someone else quipped. "Well, you all know I can't eat my chicken without my potato salad," a cousin standing in the doorway, one foot on the bus step, one foot on the sidewalk, comically shouted out. This friendly back and forth bantering was shared on those hot summer days in the late 1970s and early 1980s as we waited on the big commercial bus near 125th street in Harlem to head out to one of the local beaches or amusement parks. My grandmother Sue always organized great family bus rides—good food, good music, and good fun. The roll call of Queens, Bronx, Brooklyn, Manhattan, and New Jersey friends and relatives always managed to bring laughter, drama, and pleasure. These yearly outings were some of the highlights of our summers growing up. So, overhearing that phone call when my father responded, "Ok dear, I understand, we'll be up there soon," I knew in my heart that God had called my Grandma Susan home. We were sitting at the table in Charleston, SC, quietly eating dinner, with the television on when the phone rang. The sign of death seemed to be in the air as we each ate our barbeque chicken, red rice, green beans, toss salad, and hot buttered biscuits. Two others in our family were already fighting for their lives in the local hospitals. Within three weeks, all of them passed away. I had only been home a month, just having completed my doctoral program. I did not know that death would be waiting at my door. Her passing touched my heart dearly because she was my only surviving grandparent. My mom's mother had died when we were 12 years old, and both of my grandfathers had transitioned before her, but that was a long time ago. My plan to spend quality time visiting with Grandma Susan after defending my dissertation would never materialize, at least not while she was alive. We instead were now making plans to drive eight hours up and across the winding highway from Charleston, SC, to Roanoke, VA, to her final resting place. Roanoke, located in the big Blue Ridge Mountains of West Virginia, was a far cry from the city streets of Harlem, NYC, but it was where Grandma Susan came to call home in her final days. At least she wasn't alone; her daughter Margie and son-in-law Walter, both Reverends, had moved down to be near her and care for her. The funeral that day was a mini-reunion of many who had been on those memorable bus rides in Harlem. Uncle Lewis, our great-Aunts, many cousins, and friends were in attendance. This time the chicken and potato salad were not packed for the beach or the amusement park but rather for Grandma Susan's repast to honor her life.

She lived a life that began on the dirt roads of Charleston, SC, not too long after slavery ended and one that continued in Harlem, NYC, right before the Great Depression. One thing was clear, Grandma Susan saw a lot along her journey here on earth, and she bestowed her love to many, including her children and grandchildren, who now lived all over the world. All of these loving memories began to resurface as I sat on the bed next to my Dad, whose own life was slowly slipping away. I couldn't believe that this man, my dad, Vernon, who was so full of life and energy, was now struggling even to say a few words. A few years ago, he was walking at least 2 miles a day, typing and sending email messages on the computer, posting family pictures on Facebook, and organizing his bus trips with Charleston's senior citizens, just like his mother Susan did for us back in the day. At 86 years old, he was still a fighter. Alzheimer's had so far slowed him down but had not yet taken him out. If it was at all possible, I am sure that he would be on Zoom right along with everybody else, zooming from a church meeting to a real estate or business meeting during this Coronavirus pandemic. But that is not how his story would end on earth.

Here I was sitting on his bed praying with him and for him. My dad had been admitted to the hospital three times in the past three weeks. His sister, Margie, who diligently took care of their mother Susan, had just passed three weeks ago, and now his two nephews had died only four days apart from each other, one from the Coronavirus. More relatives and more deaths felt like Déjà Vue, just as the time when my Grandmother and the others passed several years ago.

All of them had laughed with us on those bus trips in Harlem. Now any future trips to Harlem would seem so different from those fun times back in the day. As I held my dad's hand and looked into his eyes, it didn't look promising. While assisting with making burial plans for my two cousins, we decided to call hospice to see if my dad qualified for hospice care. It was a hard decision, but my siblings and I, Vernon, Jr., Derek, and Lori, along with our mother, Hortense, felt that it was the right decision. If his time was truly near, we at least wanted him to be comfortable, to be out of pain, to be free from discomfort. It was the least we could do. Friends and family called and sent their constant prayers and well wishes from around the globe. Clergy and church members called, visited, and prayed. By the time the hospice nurse came, she compassionately shared her concern. She lovingly looked at my dad, spoke with him briefly, made a quick call, jotted down some medical notes, and welcomed him into hospice. She noticed his suffering and discomfort and immediately ordered some medications. As she grabbed her belongings to go attend to another hospice patient in crisis, she said to call her no matter what time of day or night because my dad was now in her care. She wanted to make sure that he received whatever he needed. She gave us instructions on how to administer his medication if something happened before she returned. It seemed just as quickly as she left the house that we had to call the emergency number she provided us as he gradually showed signs of being in more discomfort.

As we waited, I administered the medication, which seemed to bring him some peace. He began to drift off, but we soon realized that he no longer responded as he had in the past. We waited. We waited some more. Signs of death were imminent. First, the second hospice nurse came. She held his hands and waited. We prayed. The chaplain showed up, and we prayed, read scripture, sang, and waited. His breath got fainter. His body began to get cooler. We waited and sang, "It is well with my soul and…. Great is thy faithfulness, glory is He." The lyrics brought some comfort; we sang, hoping for a miracle. We waited. 'Victory is mine,' we sang and waited. "You've given us a life, dear God that is full, and you have allowed us to live it well despite our trials and our ups and downs,".... the chaplain lovingly prayed over my dad. We stayed all night, never leaving his side.

Within seven hours, my dad took his final breath. We cried, but these were not only tears of sorrow but tears of joy for knowing that our father was no longer in pain but resting in the arms of God. I thought, "O Death, where is your sting?"

Key Takeaways:
- Love because He first loved you.
- Love your family while they are still here, and let your love be genuine.
- Rejoice in all circumstances, even death, because Christ conquered death on the cross.

Prayer:
Lord of Heaven, we lift your name above all names today. May you comfort and strengthen our hearts as we minister to our loved ones who are transitioning. Thank you for allowing us to rest in you during this time of grieving until we all reunite again with you in heaven above. We ask all these things in the Mighty and Matchless name of Jesus. Amen.

A Poetic Justice Hymn

Interceding for our sisters who don't realize the power in their voice,

Stories harboring lessons and blessings that can lead one to celebrate and rejoice.

Redeeming hope etched in the shallow spaces of even the city sidewalk cracks,

While battling crisis after crisis and praying for those angels who divinely have our backs.

We are seeking and searching for the testimonies of our sisters, stretching from the motherland shores,

Whose lives are even more valuable than any of the trinkets found in many stores.

Some who died with no names above the graves they were buried in,

But who kept their faith in Jesus, no more a slave to sin.

The one who they knew carried their healing in his hand,

And divinely brought them out of darkness into the Promised Land.

The one who sacrificed for all of us and died on the cross,

We're still drawn to lean on our Lord, our ultimate source.

Of life, liberty, hope, and power throughout our life,

This poetic justice hymn undergirds our faith in Jesus Christ.

[i] PA Announcements Study Guide - AirlineCareer.com. https://airlinecareer.com/tests/pa-announcements-study-guide/
[ii] Nkosi Johnson - Wikiquote. https://en.wikiquote.org/wiki/Nkosi_Johnson
[iii] Committal Prayers and Scriptures | Funeral Program Site. https://www.funeralprogram-site.com/committal-service-prayers-and-scriptures/

www.ingramcontent.com/pod-product-compliance
Lightning Source LLC
Chambersburg PA
CBHW072039110526
44592CB00012B/1476